The 52 Holistic Astrological Cards
For Guidance, Meditation, and Healing

The Complete Illustrated Guide
Second Edition – includes the Astrological Realms Suit

Karni Zor

Illustrated by Maya Toby

Copyright © 2015 Karni Zor

All rights reserved.

ISBN-13: 978-1511541572

DEDICATION

Many thanks to those who help and helped, seen and unseen,

mentioned and unmentioned,

who are a source of inspiration

that lightens and brightens the way.

CONTENTS

1. Getting Acquainted with the Astrological Cards 1
2. The One-Card Spread 3
3. The Four-Card Astrological Spread 4
4. Additional Readings 6
5. Guidelines for Using the Cards 8
6. The House Series 10

Card No. 1: First House 11

Card No. 2: Second House 13

Card No. 3: Third House 15

Card No. 4: Fourth House 17

Card No. 5: Fifth House 19

Card No. 6: Sixth House 21

Card No. 7: Seventh House 23

Card No. 8: Eighth House 25

Card No. 9: Ninth House 27

Card No. 10: Tenth House 29

Card No. 11: Eleventh House 31

Card No. 12: The Twelfth House 33

Card No. 13: The Ascendant 35

Card No. 14: Mid-Heaven 37

7. The Planet Series 40

Card No. 15: The Sun 41

Card No. 16: The Moon 43

Card No. 17: Mercury 45

Card No. 18: Venus 47

Card No. 19: Mars 49

Card No. 20: Jupiter 51

Card No. 21: Saturn 53

Card No. 22: Uranus 55

Card No. 23: Neptune 57

Card No. 24: Pluto 59

Card No. 25: Chiron 61

Card No. 26: True Node 63

Card No. 27: South Node 65

8. The Sign Series 68

Card No. 28: Aries 69

Card No. 29: Taurus 71

Card No. 30: Gemini 73

Card No. 31: Cancer 75

Card No. 32: Leo 77

Card No. 33: Virgo   79

Card No. 34: Libra   81

Card No. 35: Scorpio   83

Card No. 36: Sagittarius   85

Card No. 37: Capricorn   87

Card No. 38: Aquarius   89

Card No. 39: Pisces   91

Card No. 40: The Wheel   93

9. The Astrological Realms Series   96

Card No. 41: The Key   97

Card No. 42: Exchange   99

Card No. 43: Giving   101

Card No. 44: Nobility   103

Card No. 45: Abundance   105

Card No. 46: Creation   107

Card No. 47: The Gate   109

Card No. 48: Flexibility   111

Card No. 49: The Diamond   113

Card No. 50: The Waterfall   115

Card No. 51: The Lake   117

Card No. 52: Flame   119

10. Meditation and Healing Processes   121

11. The Complete A-Z Guide For Choosing Meditation Card   123

12. A Few Words about Astrology   127

About the Author   129

ACKNOWLEDGMENTS

To **Maya Toby**

who, with love and care, illustrated

the 52 wonderful card drawings.

To my dear life-partner — **Rami Zor,**

for being there, supporting and encouraging.

And to my mother **Nava Klein.**

1

GETTING ACQUAINTED

WITH THE ASTROLOGICAL CARDS

Since ancient times, people have used symbols and signs as means of expression. Their usage influences all parts of being in the human experience: the conscious mind, subconscious mind, memory, and the spiritual.

Since ancient times, people have looked to the sky and known its secrets. "As above so below," said the wise, knowing that the movement of heavenly bodies and the universe (the macro) shed light on the personal and internal processes human beings go through on planet Earth (the micro).

My journey as an astrologer and holistic practitioner has taught me that even though solutions and healing can be offered, I prefer to give people tools so that they always may be able to help themselves.

The Astrological Cards have been developed through years of

experience in working with people. They are the fruit of a deep journey of coming to understand the astrological symbolism, along with its power of forecasting, guidance, and healing. The aim is to create an accessible tool that offers a process of significant, progressive growth to the card user every time, time after time.

The Astrological Cards will launch you into the live and living frequencies of the planets, signs, and astrological houses via symbols, drawings, color, numbers, and letters. These symbols come to life and create a natural internal process, helping to reconnect to the original source these symbols came from. By that, they offer us direction, guidance, and healing.

The deck of Astrological Cards contains **four series of conduits according to the three levels of the astrology map**:

    The **Houses** — the daily experience (the yellow cards)

    The **Planets** — the various celestial channels through which human beings are influenced and act (the green cards)

    The **Signs** — the high, precise frequencies that reach us from the distant stars (the blue cards)

    The Astrological Realms – the distant area from which the astrological signs stem (the pink cards)

2
THE ONE-CARD SPREAD

For Self-guidance

The simplest way to use the cards is to call to mind any question for which you want to receive an answer, guidance, or direction. After pondering the question deeply, ask that an accurate answer be given and shuffle the deck with the cards face down. Randomly select a card without looking. Place the deck on the table and turn the card over. Reflect upon the card, its colors, and its symbols, and try to intuitively glean the answer. If needed, this booklet can be opened to read more about any specific card.

Reading for Someone Else

First, shuffle the deck yourself to connect to its frequency. Then have the other person shuffle again while focusing on the question to be asked. Ask them to place the cards face down on the table. Draw the top card of the deck for reading. At the end of the reading, reshuffle the cards to refresh and reinforce your connection with them.

3
THE FOUR-CARD ASTROLOGICAL SPREAD

If more detailed guidance or direction is desired, an expanded reading can be done. After deeply pondering the question and asking for an accurate answer, shuffle the cards face down. Select one card from each color: Yellow will be the first card drawn (from the House Series); green will be the second (from the Planet Series); blue will be the third (from the Sign Series) and pink (astrological realm) the fourth.

The *House Card* tells you in which territory the question resides: Partnership, Finance, Work, Personal, etc.

The *Planet Card* tells you which faculty is best to use or is at play: intuition, the subconscious, the brain, the emotions etc.

The *Sign Card* gives the specific character and frequency to the answer and will add important specific details concerning the issue and the nature of the direction or guidance. For example: If the faculty is the emotions — what kind of emotions? Committed Capricorn, passionate Scorpio, or tender Pisces?

The *Astrological Realm Card* will give us a developmental task we can choose to take in order to make the best of the situation.

First, reflect upon the spread of cards. Connect to the symbols, the drawings, and the colors in order to receive guidance from them directly. Afterwards, information about each card can be found in this book.

In reading for other people, ask them to think about their question while shuffling the deck. Then ask them to choose one card from each series. At the end of the process, please remember to shuffle the cards yourself to reconnect to them.

Another method: If the reading is about a particular subject, such as relationships, work, family, etc., the specific House Card associated with that territory can be pulled out of the pack (the House related to family, finance, etc.). The other three cards, Planet, Sign and Astrological Realm, are chosen randomly.

4
ADDITIONAL READINGS

The possibilities for reading and interpreting the Astrological Cards are numerous. Actually, you can think about any question for which you would like guidance and plan your own spread that will lead to the answer. You also can decide whether to use the whole pack or only a particular card series.

Here are two examples:

What Assists and What Resists?

The first card drawn, to be placed on the right-hand side, will be what detracts from the issue. The second card drawn, to be placed on the left, will be what promotes the issue. The entire pack or only the Planet Series can be opened in order to see what faculties promote or work against today/this week/my career, etc.

Past, Present, Future

It is possible to examine how a situation is developing using three cards. The first card pulled represents the past and is placed the closest to you. The second card, the present, is placed slightly further away, and the third card, placed even further away, is the future. This method can provide a longer-term, wider perspective on a particular situation, such as work, relationships, etc.

5
GUIDELINES FOR USING THE CARDS

Before engaging in any reading, meditation, or healing process, it is important to prepare the ecology of the workspace.

―――

The cards are to be put on a clean, clutter-free table.

―――

Take a few quiet minutes to prepare yourself before a process.

―――

It is recommended that you be the sole reader, as the cards become more and more imbued with your specific energy as they are used.

―――

Use the cards for good purposes, for helping yourself and others.

―――

Never do a reading for someone without his or her permission.

The Holistic Astrological Cards

6
THE HOUSE SERIES

The House Series locates: What territory in life needs to be looked at now? In which territory can the answer be found? Perhaps the question asked is about relationships, but the card pulled indicates that the real territory is identity and self-confidence (first House) or the ability to expand our horizons (ninth House).

A single card can be taken out to stand on its own, or can be combined with a Planet card and a Sign card for a full reading.

If a full reading has been decided upon, a card can be chosen randomly from the House Series, or a House card that relates to the question asked can be consciously chosen. As an example, for a question about a relationship, the 7th House card would be used to open the reading. For a question about money, the opening card would be the 2nd House card, etc. After taking out the appropriate card, the next two cards can be randomly chosen — one Planet and one Sign.

CARD NO. 1
FIRST HOUSE — POTENTIAL

The First House deals with the great potential latent within us.

Just as the bud encompasses the whole and, as yet unseen, flower, so our dormant self is within us, with its full potential, waiting to blossom and be revealed. All the possibilities are embedded within us: our talents, abilities, and any possible pathway that we choose to take.

The card of the First House speaks about our Essence—about our inner selves—before any choice has been made. Within this potential is great power and strength.

This card points to self-reflection, even if the question relates to another person or issue. It tells us that our dealings are, first and foremost, with ourselves and we must examine ourselves closely—our talents, inclinations, genuine desires, and motivations.

This card can be used as an opener in a full reading to discover our potential, our inner essence, and the inner source of our power.

A meditative process with this card will help in connecting us to our inner power source, to the potential that is lodged within, that then helps us to radiate who we truly are.

Affirmation:

All the possibilities are embedded within me.

CARD NO. 2
SECOND HOUSE — THE TANGIBLE

This card locates us in the material and physical world. It speaks of being grounded, realistic, and practical.

This card is about how we relate to our property, money, house, and body. It reminds us to realize the abundance we live in and take care of it a sustained manner. It speaks about success and stability.

The Second House Card is an excellent indicator if it turns up after a question is asked about finance or business. If the question is about love, this card speaks of stable love, long-term and sensual. If the question is abstract or spiritual, this card grounds us, asking us to be realistic, to check the details and logistics, and to examine how realistic the situation is.

The card can be used as an opener for questions about money, possessions, assets, home, and body.

A meditative process with this card connects us to the right attitude towards the physical world, money, body, and property. Looking at the card increases the opportunity for a sense of stability and abundance.

Affirmation:

I am taking care of what is really important in a sustained manner.

CARD NO. 3
THIRD HOUSE — COMMUNICATION

The Third House examines the way we communicate with the surroundings and the way we weave the fabric of our social connections.

If asking for guidance, this card is a reminder that man is a social creature, surrounded by people. A great part of our life involves communicating in society. This card asks us to look at how we explain ourselves and our ability to form relationships.

If the question deals with earning a living, the card indicates a need for more marketing and advertising. If the question deals with a romantic issue, it speaks of social relationships (rather than romantic ones). If the question is about family matters or relationships with colleagues, this card recommends better communication.

The card can be used as an opener in a full reading to clarify something about friends or to get guidance on how to speak, converse, or approach people.

A meditative process with this card helps in developing better social connections and assists in finding more effective means of communication.

Affirmation:

I find ways of developing my social connections.

CARD NO. 4
FOURTH HOUSE — FAMILY

A significant proportion of our motivating psychologies originated in early childhood and family. This card examines the territory of the family we grew up in and the family we created. It also is connected to our past, especially the emotional past carried up to this day.

It suggests going back to childhood memories, to our mother's and father's house. It asks us to meet anew with that small child within us — and his or her needs and desires. It asks us to act with family warmth and to demonstrate balanced, confident parenting.

This card hints that the solution to any problem is in our emotional approach, which reflects the childhood we had.

This card can be used as an opening card to ask questions about family, familial perceptions we have, or our childhood experiences. This card can help guide us on how to act with our children or our parents.

A meditative process with this card will help heal the little child within us and overcome unfortunate childhood memories. It also will help us give and receive warm family feelings.

Affirmation:

The family is a sanctuary

and a place to build a loving and confident mutuality.

CARD NO. 5

FIFTH HOUSE — SELF EXPRESSION

The Fifth House deals with the way in which we express our potential and how our inner richness is released to the world.

It deals with all those things we love to do and the gifts and talents with which we are blessed. It reminds us of our ability of self-expression in a creative way.

The Fifth House encourages us to radiate and shine, and to enjoy and live life to its fullest.

This is a most positive card to any question asked because it speaks of expressing outwardly our inner world in a powerful, yet enjoyable, fashion.

This card can be used as an opener in order to discover the way to fulfill our potential and uncover our talents.

We can use this card for meditation in order to enrich creativity, add joy and energy to our lives, and radiate our full potential.

Affirmation:

I express my potential

and let my inner richness be released to the world.

CARD NO. 6

SIXTH HOUSE — MAINTENANCE

The Sixth House speaks of daily life filled with all its small details. It tells about service and the ability to act according to what the situation calls for. It speaks about doing the task and the ongoing management in life.

The Sixth House is the realm of "behind the curtain" of all the big events. For every tower, there are platforms that need to be built and floors that need to be washed. For every wonderful initiative, there are bureaucratic details that need to be taken care of.

If this card presents itself randomly, we must put aside fantasy and emotion and, instead, take care of all those little technical arrangements. All the small details comprising the whole picture, all the bills and bureaucracy, are to be taken care of, including our health.

This card can be used as an opener to ask questions about health, management, organizing the house, the way in which to maintain a business, etc.

Meditation upon this card helps us function better in our daily lives and to be in better harmony with Nature and the different tasks and duties of life.

Affirmation:

In focusing on service, I am in harmony with Nature.

CARD NO. 7

SEVENTH HOUSE — RELATIONSHIPS

The Seventh House deals with intimate relationships. It puts us in the territory of love and partnership.

Our relationships are the place where our world meets the world of others. The journey into a fulfilling relationship, whether in marriage or any partnership, confronts our identity and ego.

In this, there is an important lesson about becoming attentive to another's feelings and needs.

Love is not a luxury! It is a basic need of existence: to be in a mutual engagement and to live happily ever after in a relationship that develops and enhances as time goes on.

This is an excellent card to be pulled randomly after asking a question about love.

If a question on non-intimate matters was asked, as in work-related questions, this card suggests working with another person or a team. Another avenue of possible approach is to include and involve our life-partner in the matter, and/or bring to bear qualities of our attitude towards relationships (such as warmth, forgiveness, etc.) to help solve the issue.

This card can be used to meditate upon in order to repair unwanted patterns to do with love relationships and other partnerships. Healing our perceptions concerning love will allow us to find a new partner or to improve the relationship in which we are now.

Affirmation:

My ability to love and be loved

develops and enhances with time.

CARD NO. 8

EIGHTH HOUSE — SPIRITUAL PORTAL

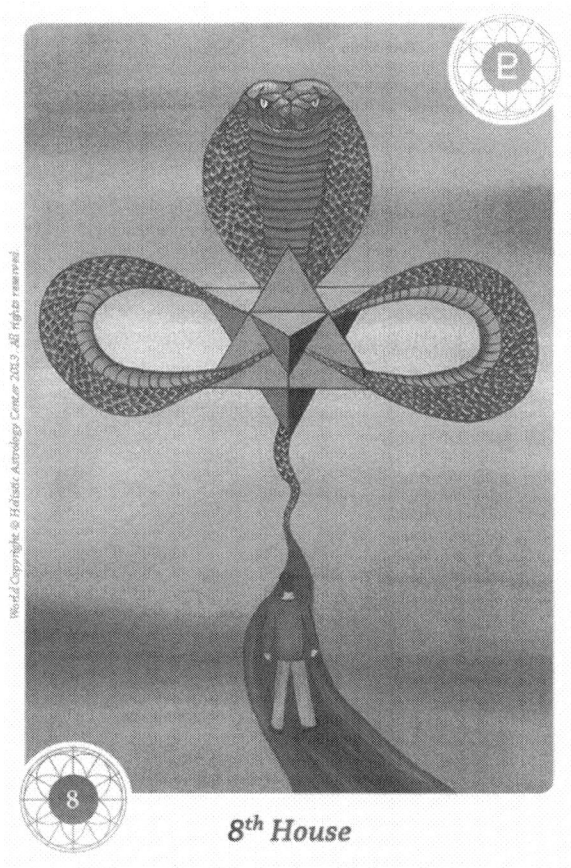

8th House

This card is special because it is attached to a dimension higher than the arena of everyday happenings. It connects us to high spiritual realms that are outside the usual perception of reality and time. It allows connection to higher consciousness, to the magic and mystery that motivate the world, allowing us to receive guidance from higher sources.

The Eighth House points to spiritual development and to a higher view about a situation. It intimates that the solution is not in the physical domain but rather in the domain of the spirit and the way we perceive reality.

This card can be used to open with in order to connect to an elevated perspective for a higher view and understanding.

It is highly recommended to use this card for spiritual meditation that will connect to higher realms and allow us to meet the higher consciousness of existence.

Affirmation:

I allow myself to receive guidance from higher sources.

CARD NO. 9

NINTH HOUSE — EXPANDING HORIZONS

The Ninth House is the journey into expanding our knowledge and letting us flourish by going out into the wide world. It provides us with experience and growth, although not yet with practical results.

As an opener, this card can be used for guidance about studies, travel, and connections abroad, as well as any area through which our scope and range can expand.

If the Ninth House card is drawn in a reading relating to any question about studies or travel, it is a most positive sign, expressing success in these areas. With other questions, it tells there still is a way to go in our development, with much to learn before the subject we are interested in can manifest (whether it be love, work, or family), but still will give a good hint for success in the future.

Meditating on this card will facilitate expansion of our views and horizons and will help us absorb the world's riches with open arms. This is a wonderful card to meditate upon during examination time to increase the ability to retain new knowledge.

Affirmation:

I am open to absorb the world's riches with open arms.

CARD NO. 10

TENTH HOUSE — WORK

The Tenth House deals with the ability to work in a steady and stable fashion over the years, and to develop ourselves, as well as our careers. Within this, qualities such as consistency, determination, and the ability to act within an orderly framework of time and rules are called for.

This card can be used as an opener for guidance about our workplace, profession, or career from the most physical, practical standpoint.

It guides us into dedication and constancy, and to work diligently through time. It speaks of something reliable, slowly developed.

It is a promising card to draw after asking a question about our work place, career, or the possibility of receiving a promotion.

Meditating on this card encourages determination and consistency in the world of work and career, and promotes action within the framework of time or under the pressure of producing results. It can also repair misaligned thought patterns concerning work, and impart a healthier view about career.

For those who are looking for employment, or find it difficult to be consistent at work, it is especially recommended to engage in a daily process with this card.

Affirmation:

I am consistent and determined.

CARD NO. 11

ELEVENTH HOUSE — VOCATION

It can take someone a lifetime to understand what his or her vocation is. This is the most significant thing we came to this world for and, when living it, we touch most meaningfully the lives of other people and contribute to them in their life's journey, thereby assisting the evolution of humanity and the world.

For any question asked, this card hints that the subject asked about is connected, in some way, to our destiny and has a purpose higher than meets the eye.

The Eleventh House card can be used to examine what our vocation is or assay new directions, developments, and progress concerning our vocation. This card can be used to get in touch with the higher purpose of any subject.

Meditating upon this card allows connection to our vocation and destiny and helps us to better focus on the higher purpose of life. It can help to open up other points of view about our aims and gives a higher perspective about anything with which we are dealing.

Affirmation:

I am on the path of fulfilling my true vocation.

CARD NO. 12

TWELFTH HOUSE — TRANSCENDENCE

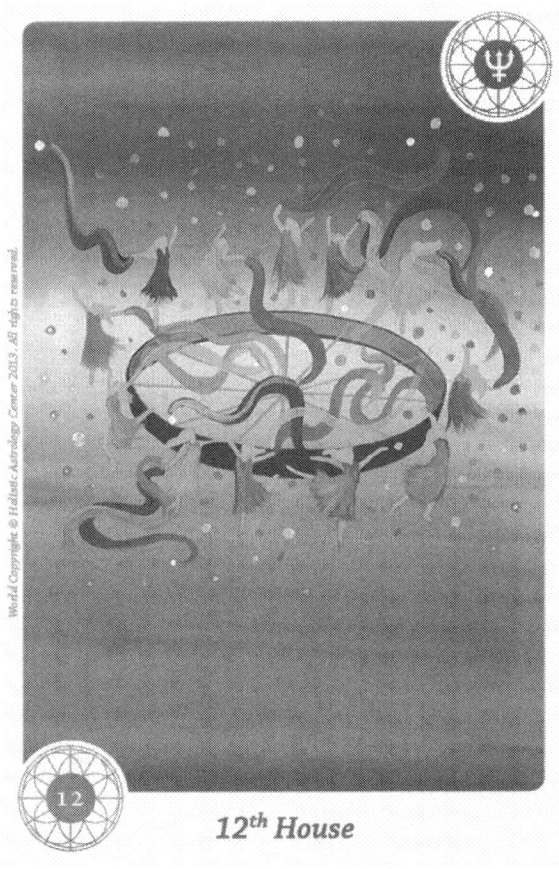

12th House

The Twelfth House deals with what is unseen: Inspiration, imagination, intuition, and connection with all things spiritual. These are the substances that will remain forever and that also will be available to us after we part from our physical bodies.

The ability to connect to these higher worlds isn't always possible. It depends upon spiritual development.

If this card was drawn randomly, it says that what we are searching for isn't found in the physical world. It speaks about something higher and spiritual, not manifest, not acquired. It speaks about intuition and inspiration.

This card can be used as an opening card to investigate the unseen worlds that move the seen world, or for any question dealing with imagination, inspiration, muse, or spirituality.

Meditating upon this card connects us to the refined worlds of spirits, fairies, angels, and muses. It improves our imagination and spiritual abilities and helps us connect to fine domains beyond time and space.

Affirmation:

I seek connection to the refined worlds

of fairies, angels, and muses.

CARD NO. 13

ASCENDANT — THE HORIZON

The Ascendant card describes the moment of meeting something new. It speaks of how we meet life's events or new people, and of our first spontaneous responses. It urges us to be open to new situations, welcoming the incoming future.

The Horizon is an exciting place where we meet new possibilities and things we haven't yet met; but if we have doubts or fears, it can be a frightening place to visit.

This card can be used in opening a full reading for deeper understanding of the way in which we meet new things. This card also can be used before a new circumstance or situation in order to receive more information about it (through the other cards in the reading).

It is recommended to meditate upon this card before entering unfamiliar places or situations. We also can use it if we want to change the way in which we meet the events in our lives.

Affirmation:

I welcome the incoming future.

CARD NO. 14

MID-HEAVEN — MATURITY

Mid-Heaven

The Mid-Heaven card speaks about the journey of maturity.

Each person has his or her unique moment of growing up, marking the transition from someone who relies on others to someone who stands firmly on his or her own account.

Sometimes it is not a specific moment but rather a continuous process.

For one person, maturity will be in holding a steady job. For another, maturity can mean developing a sense of humor. And for yet another, maturity can mean to know how to love.

The process of maturing means, amongst other descriptions, to leave behind a limited and limiting condition and to move into a wide-ranging variety of opportunities.

If this card is pulled randomly, it tells of the need to mature, develop, and grow in the area asked about. It is recommended to continue the reading and open a Planet Card and a Sign Card to understand the route to take in this journey of maturity in the specific area.

Used as an opener, it aids in understanding the process of maturity that we undergo in our lives or in a specific area (such as relationships or work).

Meditating on this card will help us to slowly go through a process of moving from dependence to finding the stability and confidence of our own principles.

Affirmation:

I leave behind limiting conditions

and move into a wide-ranging variety of opportunities.

The Holistic Astrological Cards

7
THE PLANET SERIES

Man is multi-featured. A wide variety of modes exist through which we can perceive and act. The Planet Series shows which parts of us we use or can use from the various possibilities available: The emotions conduit (Venus), thought conduit (Mercury), action conduit (Mars), healing conduit (Chiron), etc. Each of these conduits is represented in the astrological map as one of the heavenly bodies in our solar system.

For a full astrological reading, the Planet Card is dealt second after having first placed a House Card on the table. One of the Sign Cards will be put as the third card, completing the reading.

In a full reading, the Planet Card tells us which conduit is best to use. The Sign Card, which comes after, will give the specific nature. For example, Venus indicates using the conduit of the emotions. The Sign Card, let's say Aries, will speak of passionate feelings; Scorpio will speak of deep feelings, etc.

It is possible to draw one of the Planet cards on its own for guidance, advice, or direction. In this instance, the card takes on a wider, fuller significance as shown in the contents of this chapter.

CARD NO. 15

THE SUN — THE CONSCIOUS

The Sun

The Sun is the only ruler of the day, the center of our solar system, around which all the other planets rotate. The Sun represents our eternal radiating essence, our ambitions and desires that steer our conscious path. We drive the chariot of our lives and when our desires are clear, our entire life lines up in order to arrive where we are aiming.

The Sun advises that we focus our awareness and be decisive about what we desire for ourselves and others. Defined and stable aims are to be determined, and then we are to "go for it". This card indicates that the territory being asked about is central and significant in our lives, around which many other things orbit.

The card asks us to use our conscious awareness and ambitions and to radiate outwardly with the full power of the principle of our lives.

This card can be meditated upon in order to concentrate our desires and ambitions into a unified light beam and radiate it out from within. What is radiated clearly will manifest in our lives.

Affirmation:

I am the driver of the chariot of my life.

CARD NO. 16

THE MOON — THE SUBCONSCIOUS

The Moon represents all those powers, external and internal, that pull and control us without our being aware of it. It represents the world of the Subconscious, deep psychologies, the hidden recesses of the soul, the basic instincts, and the emotions.

The Moon also is a symbol of the natural feminine monthly cycle and is associated with young children, the child within, and pregnancy. It is beneficial to have that in mind while reading the card.

The Moon symbolizes deep attraction that comes from the subconscious, caused by instinctive, intuitive, or psychological motives we are unaware of. This card indicates that there are hidden causes, positive or negative, navigating for us.

If guidance was asked for, this card prompts using that force of attraction or natural intuition, even if things aren't logical or don't seem to fit with the identity we want to adopt.

Reflecting upon this card will assist in entering a more intuitive, primal, yet soft and receptive state. It will enhance our natural, basic instincts and clean our emotions.

Affirmation:

I trust my instincts and intuition.

CARD NO 17

MERCURY — THOUGHT

Mercury, in Roman mythology, is the nimble messenger of the gods, clever and fluent.

The Mercury card symbolizes the conduit of thinking and the ability to communicate. Mercury asks us to use our intelligence and to glean more information.

It asks that we implement logic and wisdom, and guides us to use our communication talents in the best way possible. It calls upon us to use common sense and reason.

If the question asked was about love or work, it calls for more consideration, more reasoning, and more conversation.

This card can be meditated upon to create mental clarity or to develop the art of conversation, rhetoric, and lecturing. This is a wonderful card for students to reflect upon before an important lesson or test. Lecturers, teachers, and public speakers can meditate upon it before delivering their messages. Reflecting on this card develops the left hemisphere of the brain.

Affirmation:

I am focusing my thought.

CARD NO. 18

VENUS — FEELINGS

Venus is the Roman goddess of beauty, harmony, and love, representing the glorious essence of femininity and womanhood.

Venus represents our ability to feel. It asks us to feel and express those feelings in a flowing, soft, and open way.

The Venus card shows us the way into a pliable and fluid inner world of feelings and opens before us the ability to love and receive love.

This is a great card if picked as an answer to a question whose topic is marriage, love, or relationships.

Meditating upon this card helps to cleanse lower emotions, connect to higher and nobler feelings, and expand our ability to love and be loved.

If one wants to open a conduit of love in their life, to heal their relationships, or to draw in new love, they may choose to meditate upon this card in a steady, regular way.

Venus connects women to the wellspring of womanhood, beauty, and softness, and offers discovery of the wonders of the essence of femininity.

Affirmation:

The flow of my feelings allows them to cleanse.

CARD NO. 19

MARS — ACTION

Mars is the Roman god of war. It symbolizes the masculine essence: direct, practical, active, fetching, defending and protecting, bursting with strength. Sometimes, when not handled well, Mars' red energy can find its way out as aggressive and attacking.

Mars indicates the imperative to act and do.

The red planet Mars symbolizes our ability to express things, moving from feelings (Venus) and thought (Mercury), outwards to action.

Mars calls for being practical and determined, setting goals and then "taking them by storm".

This card indicates that any territory asked about is very active and dynamic, and calling for expression in deeds.

This card brings with it a masculine spirit—relevancy and directness, not considering anything other than the goal.

It is recommended to look at the card for a while before setting out to do anything that requires a lot of strength and determination. This card will pulse energy and ambition through us, igniting us into action.

For men, this card strengthens the masculine frequency.

Affirmation:

I am capable. I have the ability to do.

CARD NO. 20

JUPITER — GROWTH

Jupiter is the biggest planet in this solar system. The god Jupiter is the head of the pantheon of Roman gods — the greatest of them all. Frequencies of the high and the sublime radiate from this card.

Jupiter speaks of the ability to grow, to expand scope, to reach for new knowledge, and to arrive at new places — physically and mentally.

Jupiter tells of great success in the territory asked about. It speaks of new beginnings in the most positive sense and asks that we be optimistic and open.

To be able to connect to success, we need to grow and expand, allowing in new and unknown things.

The card calls upon us to use our ability to expand beyond our own limitations.

Meditation upon the Jupiter card is beneficial for strengthening optimism. It is a good card to meditate upon for anyone who wants to grow and expand in any territory.

Jupiter also has the frequency of a lucky charm, prodding more of life's little "coincidences" to appear in our lives.

Affirmation:

I am allowing myself to grow and expand. I let success in.

CARD NO. 21

SATURN — CONSTRAINTS

Saturn is the big restrainer and Lord of Karma.

The card's message to us is that we are all here under different laws that constrain us, with rules and limitations that cannot be escaped.

Saturn speaks about something that is limited, confined, slow, and found within an inflexible framework. It speaks about rules and regulations to be obeyed. It asks that we adhere to principles, values, and morality.

This card says that to move through difficulties, we first need to learn about them and deal with them to become stronger.

The card refers to the image of the mature and responsible adult within.

Saturn calls upon us to employ values and a moral sense. It asks that we place limits and curtail activities.

For many questions asked, Saturn's answer to us would be, "NO".

Meditating upon this card can help in managing the difficulties and limitations in our lives. Reflecting upon this card will bring us to a process in which the lessons hidden behind the difficulty can be seen. By uncovering the lesson and dealing with it, the difficulty becomes another stone that builds our foundation.

This card is good to look at for those who find it difficult to say "no" and to stick to their inner values, perhaps from the worry of what society may say, or because of the desire to please. This card helps us to connect to our ability to negate.

Affirmation:

By uncovering the lesson and dealing with it,

the difficulty becomes another stone that builds my foundation.

CARD NO. 22

URANUS — HIGHER KNWOING

Uranus

Beyond the ability to think logically, there is the possibility of clear knowing that comes from a brilliant, genius higher source.

Uranus, one of the distant planets, not seen by the naked eye, allows us connection to the higher mental realms, sourced outside of our solar system.

The planet Uranus is named after the primal creator god who, after giving birth to life, also destroyed most of his creations. It speaks about a higher octave of our mental ability and the ability of creating "something out of nothing".

It hints of something original, unique, and unusual. It encourages originality and independence, the creation of something new, and the breaking from routine.

Uranus sometimes can symbolize instability, like the element Uranium, named after this primal god. Not everything created under Uranus' influence will be durable over time.

Meditating upon this card will help in connecting to higher mental abilities and to the ability to receive sparks of genius and absolute Knowing. Reflecting upon this card assists in getting out of the box of routine to be more original, and in enhancing our uniqueness.

Affirmation:

I let creativity in.

CARD NO. 23

NEPTUNE — INTUITION

Deep waters represent noble, high emotions that are ruled by Neptune, the mythological god of the seas. In these magical waters, where mermaids and sirens reside, we can find the spiritual connection to muses and inspiration to discover the greatest hidden treasures.

The Neptune card brings in a meditative dimension that's not logical. It places us in a world that is creative, spiritual, and imaginative.

Neptune asks us to connect to the right hemisphere, the intuitive side of the brain, in order to release control and let the wonders of the spirit, imagination, and creativity take the lead.

This card encourages being carried away, swept away, and confused, intuitively feeling that something higher now is guiding us.

Meditating upon this card helps in connecting to the higher realms of inspiration, making it easier to be freed of the ropes of logic into the pleasant flow of the natural intuitive realms.

Affirmation:

I am placing myself in a world that is

creative, spiritual, and imaginative.

CARD NO. 24

PLUTO — METAMORPHOSIS

Pluto, the most distant planet of our solar system, allows us connection to distant sources of pure power arriving from outside of our solar system.

Pluto, named after the god of the Underworld, represents a great magnetic power that can drag us down to scrape bottom or raise us up to reach complete revelation. It speaks of an extreme situation, and it seems that both ends are tied together.

Pluto kept two houses—one in the land of the dead, the lowest place (in all meanings), and the other on Mt. Olympus, the highest place of all (physically and spiritually).

Only by passing through the Underworld can Pluto come to its second home — elevated, enlightened Mt. Olympus.

If Pluto is the card that came out as an answer to your question, it is a big warning sign. Pluto warns of a complicated situation that could pull us down even into obsession. It is recommended to not enter situations where Pluto visits. Due to the powerful magnetic pull of the issue, it is a difficult caution to follow.

If already in such a situation, the only way to deal with Pluto is to meet the adversity head on, with a lot of strength and determination, to completely transform ourselves and our consciousness from one end to the other so that the particular territory no longer controls us. It is upon us to move through the difficulty to the other side — enlightenment.

It is a most powerful card that asks us to use the most focused strengths, ambition, and drive towards the mission. It asks us to truly transform.

Meditating upon this card can assist in passing through difficult and extreme situations, coming out the other side transformed and enlightened. It also can assist in getting in touch with our most concentrated inner powers.

Affirmation:

I am in touch with my most concentrated inner powers.

CARD NO. 25

CHIRON — HEALING

Chiron was a mythological Centaur who was born crippled and left by his tribe to die. Through the favor of the gods, he received gifts that led him to a new destiny and a new life as a healer.

Chiron tells the story of the "wounded healer" who, by overcoming his injury, gained the ability to heal others.

It is important to remember that the wound of which Chiron was healed is an inseparable part of his being a Healer. Without it, he wouldn't be where he is today.

Chiron describes a situation that holds healing for us or for others. If asking for advice, Chiron speaks of the need to heal ourselves, others, or the situation. It also reminds us that we have the ability to do so.

If asking about career or vocation, Chiron directs us to work related to healing. If asking for guidance about marriage, family relations, etc., this card indicates there is a healing process to undergo.

In reflecting upon this card, Chiron connects us to healing essences and assists in bringing relief to many kinds of pain and wounds—physical, mental, and emotional. When ill, it is recommended to place this card at the bedside and look at it frequently.

Affirmation:

I am in touch with my healing powers.

CARD NO. 26

TRUE NODE — THE DRAGON'S HEAD

True Node

Before being born, we choose the lessons that our soul will go through in its journey of initiation. The True Node, also called "Dragon's Head" in some cultures, shows those lessons and territories in which most of the struggles will occur.

These are the same territories that hold for us the most precious treasures.

The Dragon's Head suggests that the subject asked about is connected to the deep lesson of our life that our soul wants to develop by moving through that difficulty. The journey towards the solution can be long and complicated—yet unavoidable. The lesson is necessary for building ourselves up, and moving through it brings real growth, with the results remaining even after the end of our mortal life. It also speaks of breaking through into new ways and recommends not using old patterns.

This card asks us to view things from a higher perspective and to see the wider lesson at play. It puts the subject on a higher plane and reminds us that our life is just one piece in a continuum of many lives. We are a part of a bigger being than what is known in this reincarnation.

Reflecting upon this card aids in receiving that higher view needed in order to see our life as part of a greater wheel of reincarnations and to acquire the tools to deal with the lessons that challenge the soul.

Affirmation:

I am aiming to receive the higher view needed

in order to see my life as part of a greater picture.

CARD NO. 27

SOUTH NODE — THE DRAGON'S TAIL

In the long journey of the soul, it has accumulated gifts, talents, and abilities that stand at the ready in this life. These are the talents and abilities we are born with or that are acquired without any effort.

The Dragon's Tail tells that what we ask for already resides within and we just need to use it, remember it, or reconnect to it.

The Dragon's Tail points to using what we already know and are familiar with in this life or from previous lives. There is no need to learn something new — just to connect to the gifts and abilities we already have.

In questions concerning relationships, it speaks about someone already known from previous lives or from our recent past. In answering questions regarding work, career, or vocation, it speaks of using a talent already within or of something already done in previous lives or earlier in this lifetime.

Meditating upon this card allows us to remember the talents, abilities, and gifts already amassed in the wider journey of the soul, and to put them back into use.

Affirmation:

I am reconnecting to the talents, abilities, and gifts

already amassed in the wider journey of my soul.

8
THE SIGNS SERIES

The 12 astrological signs, or constellations, represent 12 frequencies, each having a completely different nature. These frequencies form a constant 12-fold radiation upon our solar system. They are natural frequencies radiating upon our planet and always within us, available for us to choose from and connect to. The signs are the highest and purest signals out of the three series, originating from a far and high domain.

In a full reading of three cards, a Sign card is the last card drawn from the pack and the last card read. It will give the precise nature of things. If, for example, the territory being dealt with is relationships (Seventh House), and the channel to be used is that of the feelings (Venus card), the Sign card will explain the exact kind of feelings within that relationship: effervescence and excitement (Aries card) or deep, intimate emotion (Scorpio card)…

Each Sign card can be used on its own in presenting an encompassing message, as can be read in the next pages.

In meditation, the Sign cards can be used to instill and strengthen particular qualities or frequencies that we feel may need to be sparked or fortified.

CARD NO. 28

ARIES, THE RAM — ENTHUSIASM

Aries is the primal flame of fire bursting forth with full force, as yet uncontrolled, unformed, and undirected.

Aries tells of something filled with energy, spontaneity, and enthusiasm. It speaks about a great quantity of energy and power available to a particular subject. It calls for action!

This card advises us to act spontaneously, vividly, and with full power.

There is something to pay attention to in regards to this energy: The bursting nature of this Aries energy allows us to work in relatively short spurts. It doesn't ensure that this energy will be there for the long run.

This card can be meditated upon in order to fill ourselves with energy and living power. It is a good "antidepressant". Reflecting upon this card helps in actively breaking into new territories.

Affirmation:

I am filled with energy, spontaneity, and enthusiasm.

CARD NO. 29

TAURUS, THE BULL — STABILITY

Just like Mother Earth, a warm home, or our own physical body, the Bull symbolizes that fundamental quality that always is there and doesn't change. This kind of stability spreads an atmosphere of calm and security over us.

Taurus speaks about something steady, constant, and reliable—something trustworthy, tangible, and unchanging. It also can represent something very physical, grounded, and down-to-earth.

Regarding questions concerning the future, the Taurus card, for better or worse, says that situation will remain exactly as is.

This card can be meditated upon to strengthen a sense of stability and security, along with our ability to stay put. It also helps to be more grounded and more in touch with our body and the physical realms.

Affirmation:

There is a steady platform to rely upon.

CARD NO. 13

GEMINI, THE COUPLE — CURIOSITY

Gemini symbolizes the close connection that exists between two opposites, the tension between them, and the ability to contain these two polarities within.

The Gemini constellation symbolizes the movement and fertilization of ideas. It exemplifies the ability to contain opposing ideas, to absorb external frequencies of thought that are passing through, interacting with our own thoughts and mental prints, and even to change them.

Gemini represents the ceaseless search and hunger for knowledge.

This card asks us to be open to new, different ideas and thought patterns; to research, discover, to let things change our perceptions, ideals, and philosophies.

It gives the reading the nature of research and evolvement. It indicates a curious nature, with an attraction to a wide variety of things.

In a meditative process, this card encourages the flow of thoughts and ideas from the external world inwards and helps us through changes. When we find ourselves stuck in a mental print (opinion or otherwise), this card can help us open up to other possibilities, different to what we're used to.

Affirmation:

I am open to new, different ideas and thought patterns.

CARD NO. 31

CANCER, THE CRAB — FLOW

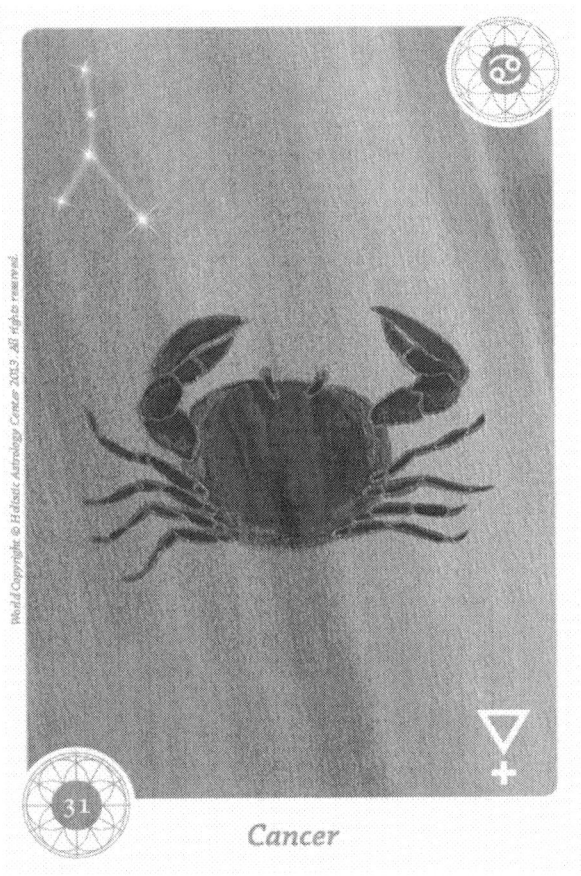

Cancer is one of the three signs of the element of water. Water symbolizes the world of emotions as well as all the water that is found in active motion all the time — our feelings and emotions that find their way from inside of us to the outside, like a mountain spring bursting forth from the belly of the earth.

This steady flow of emotions is what allows emotional cleanliness and health.

This card tells us of an active and activating situation that influences our emotions, that involves and revolves around them. According to the question asked, it tells of strong feelings directed at us, or of our own strong feelings directed at someone else or at a particular situation.

If we asked for guidance, this is the card that promotes us to express our emotions and feelings. It asks us to use our heart to come to emotional balance, to remember to release our emotions rather than suppress them.

Please note that this card speaks of the realm of the emotions — and this realm is subjective.

Contemplating this card can help the world of our emotions get into gear and become active, to help us express our positive emotions, and to release lower emotions.

Affirmation:

Like a mountain spring bursting forth from the belly of the earth,

the flow of my emotions allows cleanliness and health.

CARD NO. 32

LEO, THE LION — STRENGTH

The sign of Leo symbolizes the frequency of stable fire. The Lion is one of the four sacred animals and is the embodiment of the element of pure fire on this planet. Fire represents our energy and the Lion represents energy in its mature, stable form.

It speaks of being able to maintain a constant state of energy, strength, life, awareness, and power. The great strength arising from this mature fire invites people to join the light and the charisma it exudes.

This card tells us about a significant situation or charismatic person. It lends a noble, seasoned, energetic, and authoritative frequency to the entire reading.

It speaks of something unwavering and unchanging — yet, with this stability, there is a great outburst of power, energy, and excitement.

The sign of Leo brings the frequency of continuing passion and unending life energy.

If we asked for advice or guidance, this card asks us to be strong, mature, and authoritative — a leader.

This card is excellent to meditate upon to balance our levels of energy. Leaders can use this card to build and fortify charisma and the power of attraction.

Affirmation:

I am able to maintain a constant state of

energy, strength, awareness, and power.

CARD NO. 33

VIRGO, THE MAIDEN — CHANGE

The sign of Virgo speaks of the ability of the human to connect to planet Earth—to Nature—and to let matter get inside in order to create a change.

The frequency of Virgo teaches us to surrender to Nature all around us and, by doing so, become a natural part of the cycle of life.

This card hints of, and recommends, changes to come—changes that are very physical and practical. The "data" around us changes all the time, thus also changing us. What seems to us to be enduring is, actually, continually moving.

Contemplating the Virgo card will help us connect to the continuous movement of life, to the earth upon which we live, and to Nature, of which we are an inseparable part. This card is very grounding and sobering.

This card also can help us accept a healthier, more accurate perception of our health, body management, and diet.

Affirmation:

I activate my ability to weigh and examine things logically.

CARD NO. 34

LIBRA, THE SCALES — ASSESSMENT

The Scales speak about cognitive activity and embody the ability to evaluate, deliberate, examine, and judge. Libra talks about the mind's activity and the self-generation of thought that creates new ideas, new philosophies, and new worlds.

All is measured upon the scales: ourselves, others, and deeds in a continuous process of thinking and evaluation. And if this process of examination is not done by ourselves, then something higher will judge instead.

Libra has a cold, logical, to-the-point nature with clarity of thought and discernment that allows accuracy.

If asking for advice, the Libra card points out that the subject needs to be considered more deeply. It refers us to our mental abilities and asks that we be logical and reason with the issue from all sides.

It asks us to employ our ability to think independently and to express outwardly our thoughts and ideas that just may have the power to change things and actually create a new reality.

Contemplating this card can help develop our mental abilities and assist in activating the ability to weigh and examine things logically.

Affirmation:

I activate my ability to weigh and examine things logically.

CARD NO. 35

SCORPIO, THE SCORPION — DEPTH

The frequency of Scorpio is internalized, quiet, spiritual, and deep. It describes the deepest water filled with secrets.

All of the large oceans are interconnected and, thus, a small ripple in one starts to create a wave that, slowly but surely, influences all the others.

It speaks of our spiritual depths and natural instincts, and about that unique high place, the reservoir of human emotion, that we all are connected to, each one to each one, and from there to the sublime worlds.

With any question asked, this card tells us that things are going on at the deepest levels, mysterious and spiritual, mostly unseen. It speaks of the great powers that influence us from the depths and asks us to bring those deep urges and instincts to the highest level we can.

Reflecting upon the Scorpio card helps to connect to the deepest levels of our soul and to our higher spiritual essence, to connect to basic instincts and intuition that know better than the mind — and then use our human abilities to take that even a notch further.

Affirmation:

I connect to the deep levels of my soul

and to the high levels of spiritual connection.

CARD NO. 36

SAGITTARIUS, THE ARCHER — QUEST

Sagittarius symbolizes our continual search for energy, for sources of spiritual nutrition, and for the exalted. Sagittarius also represents the opportunity to expand, grow, and develop through that new spiritual energy entering us.

It asks us to accept things spiritual, as well as physical, with openness and allowance. It promotes growth through learning new things and reaching higher spiritual realms, and by going out into the world to expand our horizons.

Sagittarius expedites the search for additional sources of energy, for higher spiritual connections. This isn't the time to be stopped, arrested. It's the time to embark upon a journey of discovery.

It is recommended to meditate upon the Sagittarius card to increase openness and the natural hunger of curiosity that motivates the discovery of new things.

Affirmation:

I am open and allowing.

CARD NO. 37

CAPRICORN, THE GOAT — CONSISTENCY

Capricorn

This card speaks of our spirit, arriving from distant, high spiritual realms of the most intangible kind (tail of Capricorn), which seeks manifestation, to build and create in the physical world during its sojourn here on the planet (head of Capricorn).

Capricorn asks us to turn our wishes into existing reality.

Capricorn reminds us that through higher motivation, we have the opportunity to change the world in the most physical sense: To build new things, to move existing things, to create new foundations and templates, and to promote real change in the world.

Capricorn carries a very practical and initiating frequency and asks us to connect to the material world, to doing, and to reality.

This is a great card to meditate upon to direct our spiritual connections into something tangible. It also helps us develop willpower, tolerance, and constancy in order to accomplish our down-to-earth, physical, and practical missions.

Affirmation:

I am constant, devoted, dedicated, and determined.

CARD NO. 38

AQUARIUS, THE WATER BEARER — IDEALS

The Water Bearer, in service, brings water—more precious than gold—to the thirsty and tired tribe. Water is analogous to the higher knowledge that comes from the Universe to teach and progress the human race.

The unique frequency of Aquarius represents our ability to hold higher ideals and developed philosophies, all in a very steady state of clarity of mind.

In any reading, Aquarius raises the topic asked about to a more elevated level. There is a higher ideal or philosophy involved.

As guidance, this card calls for us to calm our thoughts and stick to our higher ideals and truths. It reminds us not to flutter like a leaf on the wind from here to there at the sound of every voice or opinion, but rather to find our own mental center of gravity.

Reflecting upon the Aquarius card helps us remove noisy thoughts from our brains that disturb us in our daily lives. From that quiet state, we can connect to higher ideals and philosophies that represent a truth that comes from a place higher than our own personal and fickle thoughts.

Affirmation:

I connect to the new knowledge that

wants to come into the world through me.

CARD NO. 39

PISCES, THE FISH — SPIRITUAL CONNECTION

The frequency of Pisces is soft, delicate, and sensitive. This is the frequency of a higher reality, more spiritual, that is present all the time—around and within—and that connects us to other hidden worlds.

It is a frequency difficult to connect to in the busy, everyday life. It is felt in those special moments of spiritual connection.

In the frequency of Pisces, things move slower, deeper, with a focus that is different from that of daily life. That's when what was hidden can begin to be revealed.

Pisces also reminds us to act sensitively and with empathy.

Concerning questions about practical matters (money, career, etc.), this card doesn't give an answer at the physical or practical level. It directs us to meet with the spiritual reasons and the energy source of things.

Reflection upon this card helps to slow down the pace, to enter a different dimension, to be more sensitive, and to connect to the reality of higher, more refined realms.

Affirmation:

I slow down the pace and enter a different dimension.

CARD NO. 40

THE WHEEL

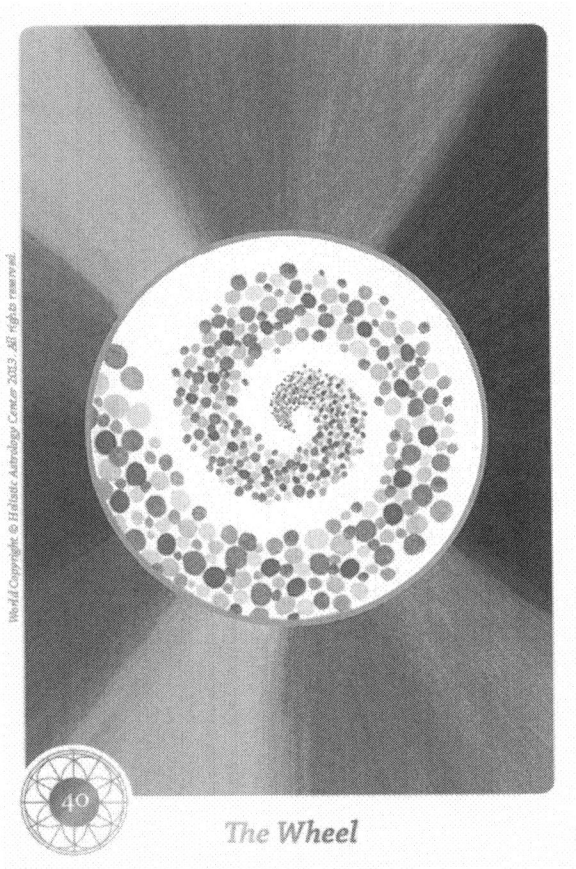

The Wheel is the Zodiac and it represents all the frequencies of the signs coming together in perfect harmony, radiating in unity from distant galaxies upon our solar system.

The Wheel card is unique. When it is drawn as a single card or in a full reading, the reading is stopped and the question is put aside, unanswered, until another time. It is recommended not to ask this question again on the same day.

The card speaks of the silence that lies in perfect harmony and intimates it is in our highest good that this topic remains without reply in the meantime.

If using the cards professionally with a client, you can use this option: Before the reading, the card may be removed from the deck and placed face up during the reading. It brings in awareness of the exalted and that not all is known to us.

If you use the cards for yourself, keep the card with the pack. It will be discovered that not receiving an answer also is a very special answer that arrives at special times.

In meditating upon the Wheel, the ability to go into the unknown is enhanced while helping us to be open to what the Universe has to offer. This card can help in widening our perspective to 360 degrees, and can be used for healing as it brings the perfect balance of having all 12 frequencies of the signs working in concert.

Affirmation:

I welcome the silence that lies in perfect harmony.

The Holistic Astrological Cards

9
THE ASTROLOGICAL REALMS SERIES

The Astrological Realms are the 12 celestial areas that house and give life to the 12 Zodiac constellations. These are 12 divine directions, radiating 12 presences that are always present, constant, and working in mutuality; 12 paths or directions, all leading up.

The 12 realms represent 12 cosmic principalities that have form in all octaves of creation.

The 12 cards of the 12 astrological realms hold 12 lessons or secrets; each one of which could be dwelled on and worked at for a lifetime.

As cards, this Astrological Realms series is the highest of the four astrological series manifesting the 52 card deck, as it represents the source, origin, and principal of the other three series, which are the Houses, the Planets, and the Signs.

At the practical level of reading the cards, this series is composed of 12 instructions for development, good advice, and call for action—things for us to do in order to achieve the best of any situation.

CARD NO. 41

THE KEY

The Key

The Key teaches us to always be in search for the origin of things. It is connected to the highest and most unperceived of all natural laws—the law of one: a law we cannot grasp, but always are searching for.

An important part of our developmental path is to learn of the laws that rule Nature, the system that makes everything tick. We should see everything around us as clues to something higher from which things originate. The research never ends, for as we develop we constantly become more aware of the next level and the next key needed to be searched for.

In a reading this card will send us to find the origin of the issue. It will tell us there is a secret, a law, a system, or a code to unravel. It will tell us we have the tools to reveal the secret by learning the natural laws.

Should this card, by the question we ask, indicate what not to do – for example, if we asked "what resists me", it would indicate not to research the subject and to keep things unraveled for now.

Looking at the card in a meditative way will help us continue our spiritual quest and will help us continue to see clues to the sublime in all that is around us.

Long-term mission: Learn the Natural Laws.

Affirmation:

There always is the quest for the higher.

CARD NO. 42

EXCHANGE

Exchange

Some of what we need and search for resides somewhere else, outside of us. If we had it, we would not be searching for it.

The exchange of knowledge, feelings, impressions, and ideas—with other people or with nature—are a major part of that which develops us. There also is a constant exchange between the seen and unseen worlds, the tangible and the spiritual—as each searches for the companionship, richness, and capabilities of the other. The longing and exchange going on, leading to a continuation of inspiration and accomplishment, allows the movement and development of life itself.

In a reading, this card will ask us to be in touch with other people, with nature, and the unseen worlds; it would suggest giving and receiving; to be open to that which is different from us and not to be fixed.

If this card answers a question like "what shouldn't I do", it will instruct us to stay put.

Meditating upon this card will help us open up to whatever wants to join us from the higher realms.

Long-term mission: Allow some quiet time for the higher things to enter and enrich our life.

Affirmation:

That which I search for resides outside of me.

CARD NO. 43

GIVING

Giving

Our true accomplishment is the ability to give away that we have worked for. If it is something we have learned, are we able to teach it? If it is our life's experience, can we give it to someone else?

In a reading, the card will ask us to be generous and give people the best of what we have. It is a great card for teachers—as people who share their treasures with their students.

If this card should, by our question, indicate what not to do, it would suggest that the issue needs some more "cooking" before being shared.

Meditating upon the card will help us recognize the treasures residing within us regenerate the inner fountain of generosity. It can be used if we feel drained, tired, dull, or if we are lacking confidence.

Long-term mission: Release that which is no longer of use for us.

Affirmation:

There always are more treasures in me to give.

CARD NO. 44

NOBILITY

As life rushes in, we need to find our inner core. The Swan teaches us the noble quietness of keeping to our course, keeping aligned, and keeping clean.

In a reading, the card will tell us to ignore outside noises and keep our steady line. It will instruct us to make no changes and continue going as planned. It will ask us not to be tainted by people and events around us, and to keep a steady core.

If this card is drawn as an answer to "what not to do", it will instruct us to be more flexible, to check our course, and listen to people around us without being vain.

Meditating upon Nobility will help us find peace and calmness and re-connect to our steady inner core.

Long-term mission: Ponder: what are the principles that guide my life?

Affirmation

As life rushes in, I find my inner stillness.

CARD NO. 45

ABUNDANCE

Abundance

Are we thankful of the abundance life offers? Can we recognize the treasures around us? Do we appreciate the multitude of possibilities?

As we enjoy the Abundance, recognize and thank god's grace—we allow it to continue pouring in.

This card will imply enjoying life's abundance and giving life to our own creativity and richness.

If it appears as a suggestion of what not to do, then it will suggest to avoid hedonism and think beyond the tangible world and our own benefits.

Meditating upon this card will allow us to better enjoy life and appreciate the abundance around us. It also will allow us to better connect and take part in the physical and sensual experience.

Long-term mission: Appreciate life.

Affirmation:

I thank the Abundance,

which reflects godly grace

and the physical manifestation of the higher.

CARD NO. 46

CREATION

Creation

Humankind has the unique ability to create new things and change reality. It starts with the power of the mind and ends with the physical manifestation of the new creation. With that comes great freedom, but also great responsibility.

This card will tell us to initiate something new, to be creative, pro-active, and responsible; to realize we have the ability to create whatever we need or want.

If this card were to answer the question "what not to do", it would imply to check our thinking patterns in order to make sure our wrong thoughts will not create a reality that is actually bad for us or others. It also will tell us not to create something new and not to go into the phase of manifestation yet.

Meditating upon this card will help us work on our thought patterns and help us make our thoughts more potent so they can create the reality we choose.

Long-term mission: Be aware of our thought patterns and the reality they create.

Affirmation:

I create, give life, and keep

that which I choose to make my reality.

CARD NO. 47

THE GATE

The Gate

Finding the gate and opening it is not the end of our quest. Now we need to go through the gate to the next level.

This is a very bright and successful card to have in a reading, but it also will remind us that what we see as success is but the beginning of a new path and it will evoke us to continue our quest.

If the card comes as a recommendation of what not to do, it will suggest to stay at the current level and not take the next step yet.

Meditating upon this card will help open whatever gate is closed for us, help overcome our own constraints, and move us to the next level.

Long term mission: Always look for the next level.

Affirmation:

I am ready for the next level.

CARD NO. 48

FLEXIBILITY

Flexibility

The Dolphin changed itself in order to fit the ecology of its choice.

In a reading, this card will remind us of the need to change, sometimes radically, in order to fit the mission we have chosen.

It will tell us to let go of what is not needed and gain new abilities, and to constantly develop and evolve.

The card speaks of flexibility and the ability to put our ego aside in order to flow with what is needed.

If the card comes as a negation, it will imply to stay steady and not change. Change is not needed.

Meditating upon Flexibility will help us go through processes of change. It will help us be more flexible as we shed the past and embrace the future.

Long term mission: Allow the path we chose, to make in us the needed changes in order to be fit for it.

Affirmation

I let the higher purpose lead my way.

CARD NO. 49

THE DIAMOND

The Diamond

The Diamond represents all that is good in us that has condensed through repetition, commitment, and a vast amount of time. These are the values we cherish and stick to without counting the cost.

This is the character we want to build and the things we have worked at during our life—and those will remain shining bright as diamonds after our physical body is long-gone.

This card reminds us to polish, repeat, and continue working on those qualities we have decided we want to have as an indelible part of who we are. It will imply a long-term commitment and will hint that there's work to do that might not be easy, but is important to do anyhow.

As a negation card, it will tell us not to be stiff, not to stick too much to our current beliefs, to be able to change position, and to be more flexible.

Meditating upon the Diamond will help us build our character, mainly through rough times. It will help us carry on in any long-term valuable and important mission. It will empower and enhance any other card we meditate upon.

Long-term mission: Work repeatedly at what is of value so it will become an indelible part of your life.

Affirmation:

I give life to the potential that resides in me,

and the qualities of my choices

by repetition and devotion.

CARD NO. 50

THE WATERFALL

The Waterfall

Part of our life's quest is to learn how to translate that which comes from the high in a way that will be accessible to our lives and the lives of others.

For that we need to become as clean as possible, so that which comes from the higher, finding manifestation through us, stays as close as possible to the original signal.

In the reading, this card reminds us of the processes of connecting to the higher realms in order to translate the signals into practicality. It asks us to focus on the mission without putting on it our own terms or interpretations, and reminds us we can connect to the higher in order to find knowledge.

If this card represents something to avoid, it will hint that it is not the time to pass on our messages and knowledge: People might not be open to it, it might not be the correct time, or our interpretation of things might not be accurate enough to deliver.

Meditation upon the Waterfall will help us become more objective and neutral so we can bring that which wants to pass through us in the cleanest way. It reminds us we are a conduit transmitting from the higher realms down to the physical realms.

Long-term mission: To be in service to the high.

Affirmation:

I leave myself behind

as I open to the future.

CARD NO. 51

THE LAKE

The Lake is inside of us and outside of us. The inner lake is the place where all our little developmental steps and insights can integrate into one big whole. The outer lake is the bigger picture, where everything is inter-connected.

This card teaches us to stay in the sum of our development, to see how different pieces connect to one bigger picture, and to see the broader picture.

If the card will turn out as what not to do, it would ask us to see the little details and not get lost in the big picture. It will ask us not to be as accepting and allowing.

Meditating upon the Lake will connect us to a higher point of view that sees the bigger picture. It will help us acknowledge ourselves as being part of something vaster, and integrate the little daily processes of development to a new steady platform we can rely upon.

Long-term mission: Integrate that which you have learned to a wider view and perspective that is constantly your companion. Realize you are a part of something huge.

Affirmation:

I take part in a bigger picture.

CARD NO. 42

THE FLAME

There is a godly spark in each one of us. This is the ever-living hope and opportunity for a new start. If it turns off, then we die. Sometimes, we need to find the way to re-light the flame in ourselves, in a project, in a relationship, etc. in order to remain bright and vivid.

In a reading, this card will ask us to find, reconnect, or re-light the inner spark.

If the card will advise us what not to do, it will call for more grounding and practicality and will suggest that enthusiasm and wishful thinking are not enough in this case.

Meditating upon the Flame will help us re-light our inner spark and re-connect to the enthusiastic inner-core. This is a very good anti-depressant card that helps revive vigor and hope.

Long-term mission: Keep the inner flame burning.

Affirmation:

By reviving the godly spark

that lives inside

I give LIFE another chance.

10
MEDITATIONS AND HEALING PROCESSES

The Astrological Cards were designed in a way that facilitates a process of healing in the person engaging them. The astrological symbols are very powerful and are connected to high frequencies of the planet, the solar system, and distant galaxies. A process can take place by contemplating upon the card during the day, or by concentrating on it for a period of time while quieting any thought and "being with" the process that the card triggers.

During any reading, it is suggested to pause for at least a few minutes and reflect upon the cards so as to have a process of healing with them. A time of reflection enables the symbols and colors in each card to resonate within you, leading to inner balance. This healing process even can complete a reading that was not fully understood or was difficult to accept.

In order to engage in this kind of process, take a break from the hurry-scurry of life. Find a comfortable place to sit or lie down. Take a few deep breaths and let yourself reflect upon a card for as long as it feels right. The process occurs while meditating, without needing to do anything special.

In addition, at any time, without any connection to doing a reading, a specific card may be selected—a card that carries a quality or characteristic that you want to strengthen or heal in your life (marriage, abundance, energy, etc.). This can be done as needed, or every morning with one specific card, or a different one each time.

In the Next Chapter you will find the complete guide for choosing your Astrological Card on which to meditate.

11
THE COMPLETE A-Z GUIDE FOR CHOOSING YOUR MEDITATION CARD

Issue to Meditate Upon:	*Number of card(s):*
Abundance	2, 45
Acceptance	9, 13, 48
Accuracy	33, 34
Action (getting into, being active)	19, 28
Balance	40
Beginnings	1, 13, 28, 26
Birth	1, 16, 22
Body (connection to, healing)	2
Career	10, 11, 19, 29, 37
Changes (being able to make)	22, 24, 30, 48
Changes (dealing with)	22, 24, 48
Character (building)	10, 29, 49
Charisma	15, 35, 49
Childhood memories (healing)	4, 16
Children	4, 16, 31
Clarity	30, 34, 38
Closing (of things from the past)	16, 27
Communication	3, 17, 30, 42
Confidence	1, 2, 27
Consciousness	15
Consistency	10, 29, 37, 49
Constancy	37, 49

Creativity	1, 5, 12, 22, 23, 38, 46, 52
Daily life practicality (dealing with, better managing)	6, 33
Decisions	14, 34
Depth	35
Determination	10, 29, 49
Development	21, 26, 37, 38, 41, 47, 50
Diet	2, 33
Difficulties (dealing with)	21, 26
Doing	19, 52
Emotions	4, 7, 16, 18, 31, 35, 39
Emotions (healing, dealing with, cleansing)	7
Employment	10
Energy	1, 19, 28, 52
Enthusiasm	19, 28, 52
Exams (passing, dealing with stress)	9, 17, 36
Expansion	20, 36
Family	4, 16, 31
Feelings	7, 18, 31, 39
Femininity	18
Focus	17
Freedom	5, 20, 36, 48
Friends	3, 30
Fulfillment	5, 11
Generosity	42, 45
Grounding	2, 6, 10, 29, 33, 37
Happiness	5, 11, 28, 31
Harmony	6, 18, 33, 40, 51
Healing	25
Health	2, 6, 25, 33, 40
Higher point of view	9, 20, 50, 51
House, home	2
Ideas	3, 17, 22, 30, 34, 46
Individuality	22, 38
Innovation	22, 46, 52
Inspiration	12, 23, 38, 39, 52
Instinct	16

Intuition	8, 12, 16, 23
Job	10
Journey	9, 20
Joy	1, 11, 13, 28, 31, 52
Karma (solving karmic issues)	21, 26
Leadership	32
Learning	9, 17, 20, 30, 36
Limitations (overcoming)	21, 26
Logic	3, 17, 34
Love	7, 18, 30, 31
Loyalty	37, 49
Management	6, 33
Manifestation	37, 46
Marriage	7, 18
Masculinity	19
Maturity	14, 21, 49
Memory (better)	3, 31, 16
Mental abilities	34, 38
Money	2, 10, 45
Motherhood	4
Natural	23, 33
New things	13, 20, 22, 26, 28, 30, 40
No! (being able to say)	21
Openness	9, 40, 42, 47, 48, 50, 51
Optimism	20, 26, 52
Originality	5, 22, 38, 46
Parenting	4, 16, 31
Passion	19, 28, 52
Past (dealing with)	4, 16, 27
Power	19, 28, 32, 49
Practicality	2, 10, 29, 33
Precision	33, 34
Pregnancy	4, 16, 31
Pro-active	19, 28, 52
Property	2, 43, 45
Quietness	40, 44
Realistic	2

Relationships	4, 7, 18. 30, 42
Relaxation	25, 44
Remembering	16, 31
Responsibility	14, 21, 49
Self-confidence	1, 19, 28
Self-expression	5
Service	33, 38, 43
Social skills	3, 17, 30, 42
Softness	23, 51
Speech	3, 17
Spirituality	8, 12, 23, 35, 38, 39, 41, 47, 50, 51
Stability	2, 29, 44, 49
Stamina	10, 19, 29, 49
Starting something	1, 9, 13, 20, 36
Strength	19, 32
Students, studies (dealing, success)	3, 9, 11, 17, 20, 30
Success	15, 19, 20
Teaching	3, 17, 34, 38
Team work	7
Tests (passing exams, dealing with stress)	9, 17, 36
Thought (clarity, better thinking)	3, 17, 30, 34, 38
Thought patterns (changing them for the better)	17, 30
Travelling	9, 17, 20, 36
True to myself (being)	5, 11, 32, 44, 49
Vigor	1, 15, 19, 28, 32, 52
Vocation	11
Will power	15, 28, 32, 37, 49
Work	10, 11, 19, 29, 37
Zodiac	40

12
A FEW WORDS ABOUT ASTROLOGY IN THESE CURRENT TIMES

Humankind, as well as the Planets, Suns, and Stars, continue to be in a state of evolution. We do know about it—but is it taken into account when approaching Astrology?

For thousands of years, people slowly disconnected from Nature. We lost touch and connection with the cyclic evolvement of the Planet, the journey that our Sun takes in Space, and its meaning, as well as with the effect the natural frequencies of the Stars have upon us.

Karni Zor's Holistic Astrology Center is integrating a new, updated approach to astrology that puts the emphasis upon the natural planetary and star frequencies and what they have to offer us in these times of transition.

The Holistic Astrology Center views Astrology as a live, mutual, always evolving process that connects between Human, Planet Earth, the Solar System, and the distant Stars.

Ancient cultures' magnificent, and sometimes lost, knowledge of the stars is taken into account, while putting aside many of the things wrongly put upon Astrology. We also are continuously doing our own research and discoveries, happy to find new and never-before-revealed knowledge.

Astrology is much more than a way to draw a personal profile and much more than a weekly forecast.

It is a natural route that converges with spiritual connection and development, a tool for enhancement and healing, and a way to remember and reconnect us to our higher origin from the distant stars.

For more information about the New Astrology, please visit our site:

www.anewastrology.com

ABOUT THE AUTHOR

Karni Zor, the creator of The Holistic Astrological Cards, is a well-known astrologist, with an ongoing column in lifestyle magazines and weekly forecasts in major new-age sites.

She has a B.A in Archeology and M.A. in Theological Studies.

Karni has been advising hundreds of people and teaching astrology to numerous students.

She has created the New Astrology method, combining the ancient practice of astrology, the current location of the stars (Sidereal method), and new knowledge that she constantly receives. She gives privet chart readings and workshops worldwide.

Karni lives in the beautiful and spiritual village of Maale Zvia in the Galilee, Israel, where she absorbs the philosophy and way of living of the Emin, some of which is embedded is these pages.

She is married and a mother of two.

Made in the USA
Columbia, SC
15 December 2020